CUSTOMER SERVICE: STUDENT BOOK

Textbook and On the Job Training Manual

From DTR Inc.'s Work Readiness Certification Series
for the second edition of Customer Service

JAY GOLDBERG

The opinions expressed in this manuscript are solely the opinions of the author and do not represent the opinions or thoughts of the publisher.

This book was written to help individuals understand and improve their employability knowledge and skills. The information detailed in the book is based on the experience, knowledge and observations of Jay Goldberg. Since hiring, firing, and promoting employees varies by company and the person performing the task, there is no guarantee by the author or publisher, expressed or implied that following everything in this book will result in a job, not getting fired, or an increase in compensation; or that employees that read this book will implement what they learn and become exceptional employees.

Contact the author, via email, at Book@DTRConsulting.BIZ. Please type "your work readiness book" in the subject line of the email to ensure that your email is not deleted as junk mail.

To order more books go to www.createspace.com/5531834

ISBN - 978-1514147290

Table of Contents

PART I

Customer Service Practices

Focusing on the Customer

I don't know about you, but before sitting down to start the learning process, I like to eat a good meal. So give me a sec while I call this great burger joint around the corner and order some food. Thanks.

I'm back. Developing good customer service skills is one of the most important things you can do to increase your value to your employer. But before you hone your customer service skills, understanding what constitutes good customer service practices, and why those practices are important to your employer, is vital.

Hey, time to pick up my food. Be right back (I know from the section *People Skills* that if I wrote "BRB" it would be wrong in a business environment).

Back again, and I can't wait to eat my burger and fries. Hey wait, they forgot the fries. You know; great food or not, I'm angry. From now on I think I'll get a pizza instead.

Let me call them and give them a piece of my mind. Want to listen to my call? Sure, why not.

"Hello, great burger joint around the corner, this is Jay, I just picked up my order and you forgot my fries." <great burger

joint employee is responding> "No, I can't run back over now to pick them up, I've already wasted enough of my readers time!" <great burger joint employee is responding> "Let me get this straight, so next time I order I will not only get a free side of fries, but a free appetizer as well. Cool." <great burger employee is responding> "No problem, see you soon. Bye."

This example shows two things about customer service. The first is that bad customer service can cost businesses money. After not receiving my fries, I was ready to get pizza instead of burgers from now on, and even if that didn't last forever, it certainly would cost the great burger joint around the corner some sales. From *Workplace Basics*, we know how important it is that the business you work for makes profits, so bad service leads to less money available for businesses to pay its employees.

The second is that if a customer has a problem, and that problem is satisfied quickly and satisfactorily, the business will, more often then not, not lose that customer. So having employees with good customer service problem-solving skills is very important to businesses. In this case, the apology (implied before I said "no problem") and the free appetizer ensured that I continued ordering from the great burger joint around the corner rather than switching to pizza.

One last, important note is that as an employee you can suggest solutions to customer problems that involve giving away merchandise (e.g. giving away a free appetizer), but you cannot make your own independent decisions to do so. Follow the company policies. In this case, if you independently decided to give a free appetizer, and that was against company policy, it would be unethical and that comes with potential consequences (fired, looked at as theft) even if done in what you feel is the best interests of the business (circumstances are irrelevant).

Good and bad customer experience worksheet

Look at your life as an example, after all when not at work, you are a customer.

Think of a situation where you experienced **bad** customer service:

What happened?

_____
_____
_____
_____

How was it handled?

_____
_____
_____
_____

How did you feel about it?

_____
_____
_____
_____

What was the result?

_____
_____
_____
_____

Would you deal with that party again?   Yes   No

Think of a situation where you experienced **good** customer service:

What happened?

_____
_____
_____
_____

How was it handled?

_____
_____
_____
_____

How did you feel about it?

_____
_____
_____
_____

What was the result?

_____
_____
_____
_____

Would you deal with that party again?   Yes   No

Now, a final question; is there anything that the business in the first example could have done to make the situation better; thus keeping you as a customer? If yes, what could the business have done? If no; why not?

_____

_____

_____

_____

Customer focus

Since satisfying customers is a key to a business earning good profits, everyone who works for the business needs to understand what service levels will satisfy their customers, and what levels of service their customers expect.

When a business gets all of its employees (including you) understanding this, that company is a customer-focused company and has a very good chance of being profitable, which keeps everybody who works for the company employed.

Therefore, to keep your job, you need to be customer-focused. Notice that I said to be customer focused a company needed to understand what its customers want and expect, not that it always had to do what its customers want or expect.

That is because there is always a trade-off between what customers want and the cost for a company providing everything that a customer wants. For example, I would love it of my cable company had a combination service person/tech assigned just to me, so whenever I called I would get through immediately and not have to listen to elevator music or sale pitches for upcoming pay-per-view events while on hold. Also, if I was having a problem, or moving, I would not have to put aside a whole day because the company said a tech would be coming to my house between noon and six at night. I would love to be able to say, meet me at my house at five in the evening.

However, it would cost the cable company too much money to provide a service person/tech for every customer. Besides, while that is what every customer would like, it is not what every customer expects. Customers expect a wait time on calls and expect a time frame for appointments. So it is up to the management at the cable company to decide what those wait times and time frames will be so that the majority of its customers will stay with the cable company (e.g. not switch to satellite), at a cost where the cable company is making profits (thereby keeping everybody employed).

So understand that every employer is faced with this trade-off decision. In this case, it is likely that shorter wait times and shorter appointment time frames would result in more customers staying with the company. However, at what cost? If the cable company has to hire ten more phone representatives to shorten the wait time on the phone, those costs will have to be made up in money earned from customer retention and/or higher fees charged to customers for the better service.

Customer service is vital to the success of a business, but every company has to perform an analysis on how much to spend on customer service based on the money earned by the company on its service delivery. This makes service delivery that doesn't cost the company anything (such as treating customers with respect, using a warm and friendly greeting, etc.) extremely valuable. Therefore, if you are an employee who can deliver this "free" superior customer service, you become extremely valuable.

Customer perceptions

A segment of customer focus that often gets ignored is erroneous customer perceptions. If the customers believe there are problems, it doesn't matter if those problems are real or perceived, they must be addressed. Only the resolution to those problems differ; not the effort in solving the customer issues. Very often, the solution to a customer perception issue is consumer education.

What follows is a true case study from the 1980's. Only the names have been changed to protect the innocent "ba; ba-ba; ba; (slight pause) baammm" (think *Dragnet* theme music)

Case study

Metrobank was one of the largest banks in the New York City marketplace. With high volumes of customers per branch, particularly during lunch time, Metrobank management was concerned that their customers may not be experiencing levels of service that was satisfactory to them, in order to keep them as long-term customers.

In order to get an understanding of how their customers felt about the service being provided by Metrobank branches, they surveyed a statistically significant portion of their customer base, concentrating on customers that had visited a branch within the last 30 days (of the survey date).

While they found some positives, they also uncovered some complaints. The most predominant ones were:

- Customers were not happy with the line waits at the branches, particularly at the teller windows. They indicated that the average line wait was about 15 minutes and indicated that a line wait of about 9 minutes would be acceptable.

- Customers felt that the tellers were often busy doing work other than helping customers, and that they should prioritize their time better, particularly when they see a long line wait during lunch hours. They based their responses on the fact that (1) they would often see the tellers at teller stations either doing work other than helping customers (e.g. talking on the phone) or taking care of personal business (e.g. eating lunch) and (2) that there were often many unmanned teller stations.

In order to study the situation further, Metrobank implemented a shopping program to determine what the tellers were actually doing and performed time and motion studies to dimension the teller line wait problem.

What they found was:

- Tellers were very productive in their jobs; they spent almost no time taking care of personal business. In fact, they often ate lunch at their work stations so they could help serve customers during their lunch hour.

- Individuals making phones calls from their teller work station was almost always work related. Sometimes they were even branch customer service reps (not tellers) that were working with a customer on a problem at a teller station to solve a customer issue and perform a transaction so that customers would not have to wait on a second line.

- On average, teller line waits were about 8 minutes not 15 minutes as indicated by the customers. In fact, only about 5% of all teller line waits were at or in excess of 15 minutes; and only about 10% were in excess of 9 minutes.

However, while the actual news was good, there was still a lot of customer dissatisfaction that, through prior experience, represented a great risk to Metrobank in terms of losing customers.

Case study worksheet

If you were Metrobank management, given that the problems appeared to be more perception than reality, would you do something to solve this problem?

Yes   No

If yes, what are some solutions you would recommend? If no, why wouldn't you do anything?

_____

_____

_____

_____

_____

_____

_____

_____

_____

_____

_____

_____

_____

_____

_____

Case study – what actually happened

The main three solutions implemented by Metrobank were:

- Metrobank invested in automated line wait equipment for every branch with even a hint of a traffic problem. The line wait equipment: (1) accurately calculated customer line waits at teller stations so the bank had a warning system in place in case line wait got out of hand (2) indicated the time of day and an approximate line wait to everyone as the entered the roped off teller line wait section thus ensuring that individuals were more accurately attuned to actual teller line waits and (3) had a clock that the customers looked straight at as they were in position to be called as the next customer to a teller station.

- Metrobank put up curtains in all teller work stations. Now, when a customer service representative or teller was working on the phone or if a teller was eating lunch at his/her station so he/she could help out during his/her off-time, they could close the curtains so that the customers could not see what he/she was doing. In addition, large branches having more work stations than would ever be used; could close the curtains at those stations so the branch did not look as if it had a lot of tellers missing all the time.

- To ensure that teller line wait remained in the satisfactory range for its customers, Metrobank initiated a floating teller pool (tellers worked at different branches each day depending upon where they were needed) to help with any real issues caused by teller absences or specific customer traffic patterns based on the day of the week or day of the month (for example a major employer in the area may have pay days on the 15th and 30th so there was a lot of traffic in that branch that day). Many of the floating tellers were part time workers who only worked four hours a day from 11:00 to 3:00 to cover lunch time hours.

- In addition, Metrobank included a note on all customers' bank statements telling them that they listened to their complaints and have made changes in the branches to help reduce teller line wait.

Follow-up customer research indicated that the measures implemented by Metrobank helped solve customer dissatisfaction. The measures employed by Metrbank solved the customer perception issue.

EXERCISE CS1

Answer the following questions true or false.

Q1. A customer-focused business gives its customers everything they want.

Q2. Providing "free" customer service that does not cost the company any additional money such as always havening its employees be courteous to customers; is very valuable to businesses.

Q3. There is a trade off for businesses regarding costs and the level of service provided to customers.

Q4. Customer-focus is a management only concept and is not something that everyone in the business needs to be aware of.

Q5. When trying to improve service delivery, businesses need to deal only with actual problems. If a lot of customers think a problem exists, but it really is not a problem, the company can ignore the perceived problem.

Q6. Often, the best way to correct a customer-perceived problem is by educating your customers so that they are better informed to what is actually going on.

*****

Your customer focus worksheet

This exercise can be done two ways. The first is to determine your personal, customer focus. The second is to determine the business you work for's customer focus. For option one, answer the questions for yourself. For option number two, answer the questions for your employer.

What follows are 30 items. The scale for this exercise is:

3 = most important
2 = next most important
1 = least important

There are 30 statements that follow. Give 10 items a "3", ten items a "2" and ten items a "1". I know this will be tough, that you may feel all 30 items are "most important." However, performing this exercise will show you, when push comes to shove, the service areas that you (or your employer) prioritize. There is a method to this madness and the 30 items will be grouped into categories later to help define your service priorities.

Question #	Rating	Service item
1.	_____	Actively seek out customer perception of the product/service provided
2.	_____	Keep complete and accurate records

3.	_____	Respond to a customer request the first time
4.	_____	Review fulfillment of customer requirements as originally stated by the customer
5.	_____	Meet all customer deadlines
6.	_____	Respond to incoming customer communications immediately, with at least an acknowledgment of receipt of said communication
7.	_____	Tell the customer what you can do for them, not what you can't do for them
8.	_____	Know what your company standards are for delivering customer service
9.	_____	Work longer hours when needed to solve customer problems
10.	_____	Constantly stay in touch with customers, not just when trying to make a sale or dealing with a customer question or problem
11.	_____	Proactively offer a response to a customer need or problem (rather than waiting to be asked)
12.	_____	Ask for customer input when developing or improving products or

		services
13.	_____	Able to solve customer problems without always having to ask supervisors for help
14.	_____	Listen intently to customers' requirements
15.	_____	Ask customers for feedback on their customer service experience with the company
16.	_____	Develop and implement vehicles to monitor customer satisfaction
17.	_____	Analyze customer complaints or problems, and learn from those issue
18.	_____	Give high priority to quality in product, service, and customer service
19.	_____	Know what the company is trying to achieve for its customers
20.	_____	Know what the company's business objectives are
21.	_____	Provide the same high level of service to other employees as you do to your customers
22.	_____	Stride to have shorter resolution times to customer issues

23.	_____	Have a positive attitude, and be open to customer comments, good and bad
24.	_____	Be polite at all times to internal and external customers
25.	_____	Strive to be error-free
26.	_____	Provide service that exceeds customer expectations
27.	_____	React with a positive attitude to customer complaints
28.	_____	Are open to change when that change will help customers
29.	_____	Looks at the company's product and service delivery from the customer's point of view
30.	_____	Know how well you are performing in terms of the company's expectations so that you can improve your service delivery when needed

Now write your results in the table on the next page (some questions will be in more than one category).

Question	A	B	C	D	E
1	xxx	xxx	xxx	xxx	
2	xxx	xxx	xxx	xxx	
3	xxx	xxx	xxx	xxx	
4	xxx	xxx	xxx	xxx	
5	xxx	xxx	xxx	xxx	
6	xxx				xxx
7	xxx	xxx	xxx	xxx	
8	xxx				xxx
9	xxx	xxx	xxx	xxx	
10	xxx	xxx	xxx	xxx	
11		xxx	xxx		xxx
12		xxx	xxx	xxx	xxx
13	xxx	xxx	xxx	xxx	
14	xxx	xxx	xxx	xxx	
15	xxx	xxx	xxx	xxx	
16	xxx	xxx	xxx	xxx	
17	xxx	xxx	xxx	xxx	
18	xxx	xxx	xxx	xxx	
19	xxx	xxx	xxx	xxx	
20	xxx	xxx	xxx	xxx	
21	xxx	xxx	xxx	xxx	
22	xxx	xxx	xxx	xxx	
23	xxx	xxx	xxx	xxx	
24	xxx	xxx	xxx	xxx	
25	xxx	xxx	xxx	xxx	
26	xxx				xxx
27	xxx				xxx
28	xxx				xxx
29				xxx	xxx
30	xxx	xxx	xxx	xxx	

Add up the totals for each column and record the results in the table below:

Column	Total*	Factor	Result**
A		3	
B		5	
C		5	
D		6	
E		22	

*add up the numbers (1, 2, or 3) in each column (A,B,C,D, E)

** calculate the result by dividing the Total (from *) by the Factor
(for example if the Total for A is 6, then divide 6 by 3 and the result is 2; all results should be between 1 and 3)

Next write the results into the diagram on the next page:

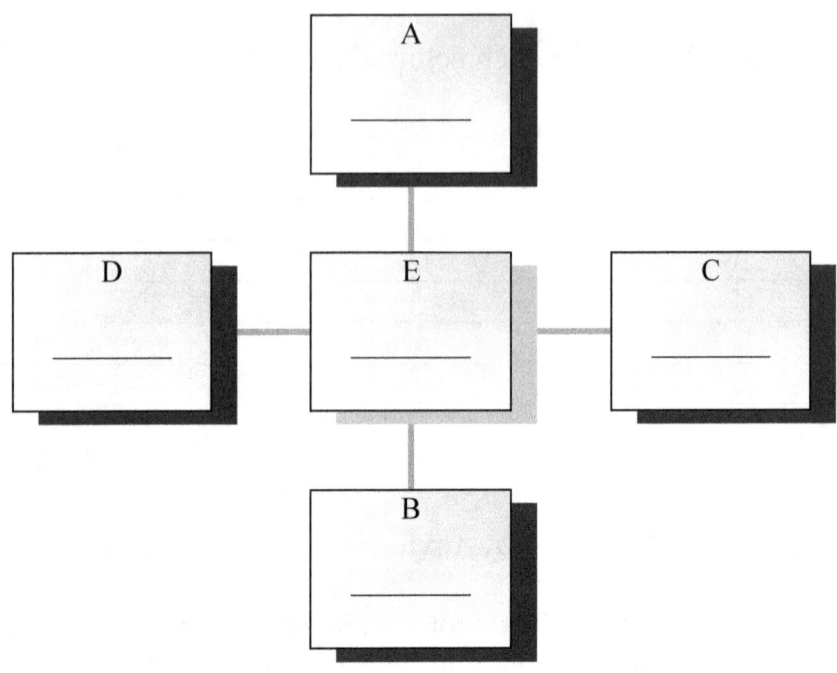

Explanation of the chart designations (areas of customer focus)

- Focusing on products and services (A)
- Delivering quality (B)
- Building the positives (C)
- Dealing with the negatives (D)
- Across the board (E)

Next copy the numbers from the chart above to the chart on the next page and you will know your (or your employers) customer service focus. The highest numbers are your areas of main focus. Your (or your company's) mission is to be very aware of situations that arise in the areas that are not your main focus, since performing well in those situations may not come as naturally for you (or your employer).

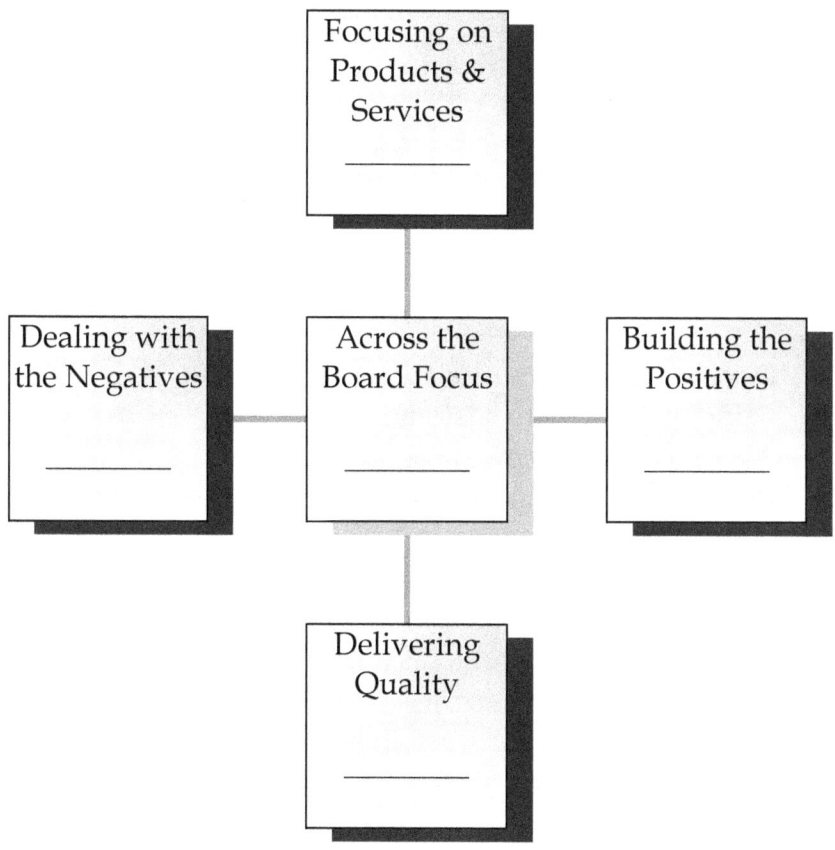

Areas of customer focus

Focusing on products and services includes:

- Good product design
- Manufactured products are up to spec (quality control)
- Developing a comprehensive package of services
- Product/service continues to meet the needs of the marketplace (solicit customer comments about the product/service)
- Make changes to the product/service to meet changing needs of marketplace

21

Delivering quality includes:

- No product defects
- High quality product/service
- Meet all deadlines
- Streamline processes

Building the positives includes:

- Developing customer relationships
- Being responsive to customers' needs
- Anticipating customer needs
- Professional appearance and communication

Dealing with the negatives includes:

- Solving customer problems quickly and effectively
- Correcting errors
- Rebuilding customer trust after problems/errors occur
- Keeping a cool and professional head when dealing with angry, frustrated and worried customers

Across the board includes:

- Has an impact on all four of these service areas.

EXERCISE CS2

Please answer the area of customer focus each situation represents (focusing on products and services; delivering quality, building the positives, dealing with the negatives)

Q1. Harvey is a top notch attorney and always provides the very best defense for his clients.

Q2. Donna is very intuitive when it comes to what the law firms clients need. She is always one step ahead of everyone.

Q3. Louis, who is great with numbers, takes it upon himself to review the law firm's accounting reports. And it's a good thing since he often finds and corrects errors.

Q4. Mike, who is a very quick study due to his excellent recall skills, has just added copyright law to the firm's service offerings.

Q5. Rachel writes legal briefs and prides herself on never having any errors and always filing her briefs on time.

*****

Identifying Your Customer

One of the least understood concepts of customer service by employees is that their fellow co-workers can be their customers as well as the people who purchase the company's products and/or services.

In a restaurant, the waiter/waitress is the worker who deals directly with the customers. A large portion of his/her income is based on tips. So it is easy to understand how providing exceptional service leads to higher earnings (more tips) for the waiter/waitress. However, the dining experience for the customers is not controlled entirely by the waiter/waitress. If the chef is slow in preparing food, if the restaurant manager overbooked the restaurant so a customer with reservations had to wait before being seated, if the bus-person cleared half the table while others were still eating, or if the food is bad, the waiter/waitress will get lower tips even if he/she does his/her job exceptionally.

In this case the waiter/waitress is a customer for the chef, manager, and bus-person. These workers need to treat the waiter/waitress in the same manner that they would treat the customers of the restaurant. They need to understand the needs and expectations of the waiter/waitress and provide service to the levels established by management. While being an excellent cook is obviously part of a chef's job, so is satisfying his/her customers, which includes both the customer eating his/her food <u>and</u> the person serving the food to the customers.

Let's look at another example.   Jane Doe works in the accounting department, entering adjustments to clients' accounts.   John Ray is a telephone customer service representative. If Jane makes a mistake in data entry, it is John who will receive an angry call from the customer. So John Ray (telephone representative) is a customer of Jane Doe's (accounting), and what Jane Doe in accounting does, has an impact on customer satisfaction, even though she never deals directly with customers.

Everyone's job has an impact on customers and co-workers. Your goal needs to be to satisfy both the external customers (people who purchase the company's products) and internal customers (co-workers who rely on your work).

EXERCISE CS3

For each job below, identify at least two other job functions within the company that the job impacts (in other words identify two internal customers for each job function). Do not just list a job title, explain how the job listed could impact the co-worker.

TIP - To help identify internal customers; play the what-if game using a situation where things go wrong.

1. You are a phone representative for a newspaper; external customers call you to place classified ads. Who are some of your internal customers?

2. You work on an assembly line putting together two pieces of a 10-piece piece product. Who are some of your internal customers?

*****

Know your customers

Whether internal or external, understanding your customers' needs goes a long way towards improving your ability to satisfy those customers. One method to help you understand your customers' mindsets is to ask and answer a set of simple questions.

1. What products and services, and support, do your various customers need?

2. When do your various customers need their products and service delivered? (This helps set work schedules and work task priorities.)

3. Where do you need to provide the products or services you provide to your various customers?

4. How do your various customers use the products and services you provide to them?

5. Why do your various customers use or need the products and services you provide?

6. The interconnectivity between "the how" and "the why" helps you identify how satisfied your customers will be with your products and services; and ensures that your products and services continue to meet your various customers' needs.

7. Who is the decision-maker for purchasing your products and services, and for determining how satisfactorily your product or service meets your various customers' needs (e.g. determining the quality of the product or service delivered to the customer)?

8. How much are your various customers willing to pay for the products and services you provide? How often do your various customers use your products and services? How much of your products and services do your various customers use?

EXERCISE CS4

Answer the 8 questions for know your customer for the following customer:

You work for a printing company and your customer is a law firm that has a standing order for their law firm's custom stationary to be delivered to them by your company every Wednesday. The order is 10,000 pieces and they pay $1,500 for the stationary that uses top shelf paper. The order is dropped off between 9:00 AM and 9:30 AM and is reviewed by the manager of Purchasing Department who signs off on the delivery.

Q1. What product and services are used by your customer?
Q2. When do they need the products and services delivered?
Q3. Where do your customers receive their products?
Q4. How do your customers use your products?
Q5. Why do your customers need this product?
Q6. What is the interconnectivity between the how and the why? (bonus question)
Q7. Who determines if your product meets your customer's standards?
Q8. How much of the product do they use and how much do they spend on the product

*****

Your job's impact on customers

It has been estimated that on average, about 23% of all employees deal directly with external customers, but on average 75% contribute to the customer's experience while never interacting directly with the customer. So even if you never interact with external customers directly in your job, there is an excellent chance that your work still directly impacts your company's customers' experience, good or bad, with your employer.

Some examples:

- The employee who writes the instructions for putting together or using a product

- The manager who hires and trains customer service representatives

- The employee who codes the web site customers use to conduct business with the company

- The employee who decides the price to charge for the company's products and services

- The manager who sets the policy for returns

- The manager who decides the pay levels within the company (dictates employee turnover and employee skill level which directly impacts the experience and knowledge of the employees that customers interact with)

- The manager who determines the marketing budget and strategy (this can determine if customers even find the company to be able to use a product or service that they need or would enjoy)

- And many, many, more

Service Measurements

Now that we all know that customer service, to both internal and external customers, is vital to everyone keeping their jobs, how does a company know if the service that is being provided is good enough to keep (and grow) the business' customer base?

The answer is by using service measurements, both from a department and company perspective, and from an individual perspective.

Many companies have quality and timeliness indicators. These include timeframes and the percentage of work that meets that time frame. For example, a company may have an indicator that states that 95% of all customer problems will be resolved within two days. Then the company puts a process in place to measure how long it takes to solve customer problems. The company hires employees who will record when every problem first comes in, and record when every problem resolution letter or email is sent out. This is not done to create a "big brother" atmosphere at work. It is done because that company's experience and/or research shows that a quick two-day resolution is the time needed to satisfy and maintain the majority of that company's customers who experience problems (note – the two day timeframe here is an example, not a standard resolution time).

However, timeliness is only half the battle. The other half is quality (e.g. proper resolution explained in a manner that the customer can easily understand). To measure quality the company might randomly select problem resolution letters or emails and have them reviewed by a supervisor. The company might also keep track of the number of repeat problems (when customers contact the company a second time for the same problem after a resolution letter or email was previously sent to them).

The key here is for you to expect that the work you do will be tracked, and that it is being tracked so that management can respond in a timely manner when they see that service delivery is at a point where it will negatively impact the company's profits and therefore, your job security. This may mean more paperwork and recording of data than you feel is necessary, but that extra work is there to protect your job.

A more personal service measurement is when your employer tracks your work. This is done so that when problems are found (e.g. there have been too many repeat problems) the company can find the cause of the problem and fix it. For example, the company may find that one worker is the primary cause of the increase in repeat problems and decide that that employee needs to be re-trained. Also, if the repeat problem is found to be from many employees, a further analysis may determine that a standard response letter or email for a specific problem needs to be re-worded.

Without tracking individuals, companies would only be able to determine when bad service exists, but would not be able to pinpoint and correct the problem.

So expect to have your specific work tracked. That could be the number of calls answered per hour, the type of problems you have worked on, the number of sales made, etc. Also know that these numbers are used to help identify and fix problems and to identify where employees need additional training help.

In addition to tracking actual work, many companies involve their customers in the service tracking process. Surveys, where customers report on actual experiences with the company are one way this is done. Another is called "shops." This is where a company hires someone to be a customer and report on their experience with the company.

Examples of Service Measurements

Customer Service Call Center	• Number of rings before a call is answered
	• Percent of time all trunks are busy
	• Percent of calls abandoned (caller hangs up before call is answered)
	• Call monitoring for proper greeting, proper procedure (one stop service, correct information given to customer, etc.)
	• Test calls to ensure proper information is being given out for specific scenarios
	• Percent of time phone representatives are off-line
	• Number of times a phone representative is late to work
	• Employee productivity measurement

Sales Call Center	• All of the above plus number of sales by product, number of up-sells, sales per hour, etc.
Back Office	• Problem resolution time frame • Correspondence sent out on time (e.g. customer statements, etc.) • Accuracy, clarity of customer correspondences • Quality control checks on correspondences (correct correspondences sent to proper customers) • Accuracy of accounting records • Delivery deadlines met • Employee productivity measurements
Retail Outlet or Service Center	• Average line waits by type of function • "Shops" to determine if the employees are either selling correctly and professionally or are providing customers with the proper information or problem resolution • Employee productivity and sales measurements
Manufacturing	• Proper safety procedures followed • Product inspection (sample finished product to accept/reject batches of work) • Machine inspection (to ensure working correctly and to ensure proper maintenance was completed • Quality review of packaging and customer orders

- Measure production output and time frames
- Employee productivity measurements

Customer Service Phone Center

A customer service phone center offers an excellent window into the entire service process.

First, one of the keys to an efficient phone center from a customer's point of view is to minimize the wait time on the phone before speaking to a phone representative. To do this it is important that the business makes efficient use of its phone representatives. So customer service phone centers run on a tight time schedule to ensure that there are enough phone representatives available to handle the expected call volumes whereby callers do not spend too much time on hold. Therefore, when management gets on a phone representative's back because he/she shows up late, or doesn't allow a phone representative to pick his/her own lunch time, or doesn't allow more than one person to leave on a bathroom break at a time, it is not that the supervisor is treating his/her staff like kids or that the supervisor is a control freak; it's that the supervisor is trying to minimize hold times for the callers.

To show you how quickly a phone center can get out of control, let's say a co-worker of yours comes in 15 minutes late (I know you wouldn't come in late). During those 15 minutes callers are on hold longer than usual because the phone center is down one staff member, so 10 callers hang up because they have to leave to go to work. These 10 dissatisfied customers are now going to call back later in the day adding unexpected call volume to that time frame. Let's say that all ten call during their lunch break. Now the phone center is understaffed during lunch because it was staffed for ten less calls than it gets. So during lunch time

35

callers will be on hold longer than expected and some of them will hang up because they have to eat. This creates more dissatisfied customers and adds more unexpected call volume to another time period in that day or the next day. That in turn will create even more dissatisfied customers and create future time periods where there will be more calls and longer hold times than expected. As you can see, this fifteen minute tardiness can result in a problem that lasts for days, and many dissatisfied customers. Now add in the fact some workers could come back late from lunch or take a bathroom break at a bad time, etc. and you see why phone center managers have to manage their employees' time very closely. So if you work for a phone center, expect your time to be managed closely and do not blame it on your supervisor's lack of respect for you or his/her personality. Know that it is because of the nature of phone centers.

However, call wait times are not the only service delivery that is important to customers when they call a company's phone center. Being able to get their question answered without being transferred from person to person, not being placed back on hold for long periods, the tone of the phone representative, etc. are all important to the callers.

Therefore, most phone centers have quality and timeliness indicators for both the phone center as a whole and for individual phone representatives.

For the phone center as a whole, the service indictors could be the percent of callers placed on hold, the average hold time, the percent of callers on hold that were on hold for over two minutes, the number of calls by hour by day (to help with staffing), the type of calls being received, the average talk time per call, surveys to determine customers' experiences and expectations, and more.

These indicators help management with staffing schedules; help management know how well service is being delivered to its customers; and provides red flags to indicate when poor service could start impacting the company's profits (and worker's jobs).

For individual phone representatives, service indicators could be the number of calls answered per day, average talk time, the percent of time the phone representative was plugged into the phone system and available to take a call, the number of calls transferred to someone else, the types of calls handled by each phone representative, and more.

These indicators help phone center management ensure that the phone center is operating efficiently and where to go to solve problems and improve service delivery.

One area where phone representatives often get mixed signals is when they are told to resolve all customer problems and then are expected to keep to an average talk time. Many phone representatives feel that if they have to spend a lot of time with a customer to resolve his/her problem, that he/she should do so. What phone representatives have to understand is the big picture. While they are providing superior customer service to one customer on a long call, three or four other callers are experiencing bad customer service because of the long hold times due to the unavailability of that phone representative to answer more calls. So use good judgment when extending call times beyond the norm, and try not to extended calls unnecessarily.

EXERCISE CS5

You start your own computer repair business. You have three employees who perform all computer repair work. You know that customers do not like being without their computers for more than a day or two. In fact you advertise that you not only fix all problems, but fix them faster than your competition.

In addition, since this is a brand new business, in six months you plan on hiring a manager to assign work, solve the most difficult computer issues; and to contact all customers twice a year to help nurture an excellent customer/company relationship, remind them of the services your company provides, and gently probe them to see if they have any current computer issues that your company can help them with. You hope that you will be able to promote one of your three current employees to that position down the line.

Q1. List three service measurements you would implement to help track the amount, quality and timeliness of the work being done by the company or by individuals.

Q2. List two service measurements you would implement to help you track who would be the best person to promote to manager down the line.

*****

Customer Service Profitability

The reason that businesses put money, manpower and resources into customer service is that superior customer service makes a company more profitable.

Old thinking is that customer service is a necessary expense. Current thinking is that providing excellent customer service is a way for a business to differentiate itself in the marketplace, thereby maintaining and growing its customer base.

Therefore, most companies measure and track their service delivery, and often obtain input from customers to see how their service delivery could be improved.

Below are some real life examples:

- Research by GTE Telephones showed "perceived service" companies can charge 10% more.

- Detroit Diesel canvassed 40 distributors, whose 250 suggestions cut deliveries from five days to three days.

- Within the first three years of its customer service measurement program, American Express cut transaction costs by 21%.

- In 1991 a large UK engineering company responded to customers' requests and issued clear spare part lists with prices. Parts sales rose by 34%.

- Citibank's strategic plan for differentiation in the marketplace (to grow market share) went from dealing with countries rather than individuals to technology (they were the first to offer cash machines) to offering superior customer service.

- Citibank's credit card division performed a customer service profitability model that showed that: (1) customers satisfied with the service provided by Citibank used their Citibank credit card about twice as often as customers dissatisfied with service provided by Citibank (those customers used other options such as cash or a different credit card) and (2) 80% of customers who had problems with their Citibank credit card but were satisfied with the service provided when Citibank fixed their problem, returned to be satisfied customers with product usage at levels the same as customers that never had a problem and were satisfied with the service they received from Citibank.

Dissatisfied customers defect, and spread negative word of mouth about the company which reduces the company's revenue. Satisfied customers continue to use a company's products and services, and spread positive word of mouth about the company which increases the company's revenue.

PART II

Customer Service Skills

Service Attitudes

Many service providers have the wrong idea about customer service. They place burdens and expectations on their customers unfairly. What follows are the "Top Ten Truisms of Customer Service." While this "top ten list" may never make it to the *Late Show with David Letterman*, it is an important list just the same. If you understand these ten truisms, you will become an extremely valuable employee of any business.

1) <u>Customers expect a lot of service.</u> As a provider of customer service, it is not your job to define your customer's need, but to satisfy those needs.

2) <u>Customers contact a provider of customer service to have their problems resolved.</u> They don't want excuses; they just want their problems resolved. If there are problems in your workplace that are prohibiting you from resolving their problems (e.g. computers are down, staff is out sick, etc.) they don't care, and why should they, that's your problem, not their problem.

3) <u>Customers expect to be able to get an answer to all their questions from the person to whom they are speaking.</u> Customers do not care if the person they are speaking to is a new employee, is in another department, etc. They want an answer. So if you are the right person, be prepared; if you are

not, know who the right person is and patiently and politely send your customer to him/her. However, be sure that the person you send your customer to can, indeed, resolve his/her problem.

4) <u>Customers feel it's their right to contact the company that they transact business with, whenever they want.</u> While this may cause extra call volume, this is a good thing for the business since it means that customers are becoming comfortable with, and dependent on it. This results in customer loyalty, which leads to more sales, which leads to more profits, which leads to job security and more money available for employee salaries.

5) <u>Customers hate waiting on long lines whether on the phone or at a place of work.</u> Having customers wait long is like telling them that you do not value their time. Customers have better things to do than wait. Try this. Look at your watch's minute and second hand. Now put down the book and without counting, pick it up when you think two minutes have passed. Now look at your watch again. Waiting makes time pass slowly.

6) <u>Customers know that they are important.</u> Without customers the business would close and you would be out of a job. So they are correct. Therefore, customers do not care that providers of service have many customers to deal with. When they have problems, they expect you to deal with them, not to be busy with other customers.

7) <u>Customers expect to be able to get quick resolutions to their problems.</u> After all, they chose to do business with your company, and they had every right to expect that <u>no</u> problems would occur. If one occurs, it is the company's fault (customers never believe it was their error, even when it clearly is, and they

have paid for the right to feel that way with their purchase), so the company should fix it right away.

8) <u>Run-around is one of the most hated of all bad customer practices and usually results in losing a customer.</u> That is why it is important that you know your job so you can resolve all problems that you are suppose to be able to resolve (or are given the responsibility to resolve) and that you know the responsibilities of your co-workers so if you must refer the customer to someone else, you are referring him/her to the right person (one who can resolve the problem). If the customer interaction is over the phone, when you transfer the call, stay on the line and inform the person of the details that the customer has already told you so he/she does not have to repeat everything all over again. If possible, do this in a three-way call with the customer also on the line. Introduce the customer to the new representative and explain the situation briefly at that time. The same thing goes for an in person visit. If possible (same building, is okay to leave your work area) walk the customer over to the person you are referring him/her to, introduce the customer to your co-worker, and briefly explain the situation.

9) <u>Customers will often try to go over the head of the person with whom they are speaking without giving that person a chance to solve the problems.</u> Like it or not, this is their right. However, your supervisor may not like taking calls/having customers referred to him/her from customers who have problems that their providers of service can resolve. A good way to handle a situation like this is to say, "I have no problem with transferring you/sending you to my supervisor whenever you want, but I would appreciate the opportunity to satisfy you by resolving your problem first." If this doesn't work, transfer the call/refer the customer. If the interaction is over the phone, do not hang up to avoid transferring the call. The customer will

just call back (still has to get the problem resolved), and in most cases, the call can be traced to you. Sometimes this happens and the employee never finds out, and wonders why he/she never receives good pay raises. Other times, the employee who hung up is called into his/her supervisor's office to explain why he/she hung up on the customer.

10) <u>Customers will often call/show up with problems that they could easily resolve themselves.</u> For example, a customer may continually show up/call for help programming his/her cell phone. And he/she may keep contacting your company to program the same feature! Once again, it is their right to do so. In fact, it may be this service feature (calling in for help) that has kept them a customer of the business and may have even resulted in a lot of referrals. As a provider of service, you cannot choose what services your customers should take care of themselves and which services you are fine with performing for them. Customers decide what they need help with and your job is to help them with all of their needs.

EXERCISE CS6

Please answer the following questions true or false. Then explain why you choose true or false.

Q1. If you are working with a customer and cannot answer his or her question it is okay to pass them off to another customer service representative whether or not that other employee knows the answer the answer since with that employee there is at least a chance that the customer can get his or her question answered.

Q2. If there is a serious customer problem going on at work resulting in a lot of customer calls about that problem, and a customer calls you with a simple question such as how to use a product feature, you have a right to tell that customer to try doing it the best he or she can and if they cannot figure it out to call back tomorrow. After all the other callers on hold have serious problems.

Q3. If a customer does not like the way a conservation with you is going and asks to speak to your supervisor; your response should be that you are the only one who can help the customer so they should relax and be respectful and allow you to fix his or her problem.

Q4. Customers who expect all their problems will be fixed with one simple phone call are customers the business should cut loose. After all, it will be impossible to always satisfy them.

Q5. Customers need to understand that phone representatives have no control over how long they wait on the phone before a call is answered so they have no right to start off their call with you complaining about that long wait.

*****

Active Listening

When you get into a conversation with one of your friends, you spend about half the time talking and half the time listening to what your friend has to say. Often you interrupt your friend because you believe you know what he/she is going to say, or because you just have to get in a comment at that specific point in time. While this is okay for friendly chats, it is not how you should conduct your conversations with customers, management, and even co-workers when he/she is explaining a work-related item to you. Even in friendly chats, I have found that when I interrupt the person I was talking to because I thought I knew what he/she was going to say, often my friend tells me that I got it all wrong. When that "friend" has been a woman I'm in a relationship with, I've heard that I got it all wrong with great emphasis and major consequences!

When interacting with customers, supervisors and co-workers who are explaining work-related topics to you, instead of using normal conversation skills, use active listening skills.

Instead of the 50% talking, 50% listening, active listening involves only 20% talking and 80% listening. Also, do not interrupt the other person. Allow him/her to finish his/her thought. Do not jump to conclusions or assume. Save your questions until after he/she has completed his/her thought. To help you with this, have a pad of paper and a pen handy. Take notes on important points. Do not rely on your marvelous, but sometimes failing memory. Jot down your questions so you can ask them at the appropriate time.

In addition, when using active listening skills in person, your personal signals (nonverbal communications) count. You need to convey to the person you are talking to that you are paying attention and are interested in what he/she is saying.

To summarize:
- Normal conversation = 50:50 (talking to listening)
- Active listening = 20:80 (talking to listening)
- Active listening deals with other's views & feelings
- Active listening requires a lot of concentration before responding
- Active listening is needed to:
  - help understand others
  - eliminate emotions from the message
  - be able to identify real concerns
  - keep attitudes and prejudices out of way
  - help decode hidden messages
- All of the active listening characteristics previously listed, leads to taking the appropriate action

Normal Conversation vs. Active Listening

NORMAL CONVERSATION ACTIVE LISTENING

NORMAL CONVERSATION	ACTIVE LISTENING
Passive	Make eye contact
May forget quickly	Keep concentrating
Doesn't fully register	Summarize to ensure everything registers
May not show you are concentrating	Display behaviors to show concentration
No notes	May make a few notes

Active Listening Building Blocks

- Attention: good posture, make eye contact, attentive silence, lean forward, smile, nodding yes, do not cross your arms or legs
- Cues: invitation to talk, infrequent but open-ended questions (e.g. tell me about your problem, what happened next)
- Reflection: repeating brief (key) phrases, paraphrasing using your own words, summarizing

Active Listening Stumbling Blocks

- Judging: criticizing, prejudices, name-calling, assumptions
- Controlling: giving orders, moralizing, threatening, know-it-all, advising (as opposed to solving)
- Avoiding: diverting, reassuring only (when there is a real problem)
- Selective Listening: hearing what you want or expect to hear, not what is actually said

EXERCISE CS7

This is an exercise to build the active listening skill of attention. The exercise is done in pairs. The exercise will be done twice with each person taking turns being the speaker and the listener.

Q1: The speaker takes about seven minutes and talks about his or her favorite movie. The listener sits and listens. The only thing the listener can say during the seven minutes are invitations to talk (please continue, go on, etc.). The listener needs to show with his or her body language (posture, eye contact, etc.) that he or she is very interested in what the speaker is saying. After the seven minute session is over, the speakers lets the listener know if her or she believed that the listener was truly interested in what the speaker was talking about. Then the speaker should say why he or she felt the listener was or was not interested. Remember to perform this exercise twice with each party taking turns at being the speaker and listener.

*****

EXERCISE CS8

This is an exercise to build the active listening skill of <u>repetition</u>. The exercise is done in pairs. The exercise will be done twice with each person taking turns being the speaker and the listener.

Q1: The speaker takes about ten minutes and talks about his or her favorite television show (must be a new topic, not the same talk as last time). After every two or three sentences the speaker stops talking and the listener tries to repeat what was said word for word. The speaker must talk at a normal conversation pace, not slowly to help the listener. If the speaker forgets to stop, the listener should put up his or her hand to stop the speaker (FYI - a nonverbal personal signal). The purpose of this exercise is to get the listener to listen very closely to what someone is saying, close enough that he or she can repeat what was said. It is not a memory exercise and will not be graded as such. This is also an excellent exercise to help build the foundation for waiting until someone completes a thought before talking. Remember to perform this exercise twice with each party taking turns at being the speaker and listener.

*****

EXERCISE CS9

This is an exercise to build the active listening skill of <u>summation</u>. The exercise is done in pairs. The exercise will be done twice with each person taking turns being the speaker and the listener.

Q1: The speaker talks in three minute spurts and talks about his or her favorite book, comic or magazine (must be a new topic, not the same talk as last time). There will be three three-minute intervals for each speaker for this exercise. After each three minute interval, the listener will summarize what the speaker just said. The listener should NOT repeat what was said word for word; and should not add any of his or her thoughts, views or comments on what the speaker communicated. The listener should just summarize the key facts. After each summary (please note that a summary is shorter than the original), the listener should ask the speaker if the listener got the key facts correct. If the listener says "no", ask him or her what was missed, and continue with the exercise. Remember to perform this exercise twice with each party taking turns at being the speaker and listener.

Helpful hint: Here is an example of a summary from a statement:

"My favorite book is *Dune* by Frank Herbert because I found the correlation between the spice in the book and oil today very interesting. I was an economics major in college and amongst other things; Dune is a novel about economics."

The summary might be: *Dune* is Jay's favorite book because of how it's relevant to today's economy.

*****

53

EXERCISE CS10

This is an exercise to put the three previous skills learned together to provide a <u>comprehensive active listening skill set.</u> The exercise is done in pairs. The exercise will be done twice with each person taking turns being the speaker and the listener.

Q1: The speaker will talk for about 10 minutes and talks about his or her favorite band or favorite type of music (must be a new topic, not the same talk as last time). For this exercise the listener will use all three skills performed in the previous three exercises. The listener will listen to what the speaker is saying; showing attentive personal signals (including invitations to talk) and will listen closely and speak only when the speaker completes a thought. When the listener speaks it will be to summarize what was said, using a key word or phrase in the exact way that the speaker said it to the listener. Remember to perform this exercise twice with each party taking turns at being the speaker and listener.

*****

The skills learned in these four exercises not only work well on the job with customers and supervisors (and co-workers who are talking about a work topic), but will also work in social situations to make good impressions on the people you meet.

Conquering Communication Barriers

Unfortunately, you don't get to choose the person to whom you are providing service. Also, in some instances your work environment may be less than ideal. Therefore, there are often barriers to communicating with a customer. It is important that you recognize these barriers so you can work around them to provide quality service to your internal and external customers.

Communicator's weakness

The customer who is informing you about their problem may have some communication shortcomings. They may:

- use an inappropriate tone or approach
- be unable to use communication skills adequately
- lack sufficient knowledge to communicate their problem effectively
- be a poor listener
- have a predetermined solution to their problem that is not a realistic solution

Receiver's weakness

The customer service representative who is listening to a customer's problem may have some communication shortcomings. They may:

- be reluctant to receive information
- not be paying attention to the customer
- be unfamiliar with the content or subject matter
- be unprepared to handle customer problems
- possess or be affected by some of the items expressed previously

Language

Language can be a barrier to effective communication. The vocabulary of both the individual communicating a problem and the individual listening to the problem can be problematic. Also, when discussing your solution to a customer's problem, be sure not to use jargon, especially not jargon internal to your company (e.g. "Go to the bank and speak to the CSR" should be "Go to the bank and speak to a customer service representative"). Finally, make sure that there is no ambiguity, rambling or double meanings in your communications with your customers.

Psychology

Individual personalities can also be barriers to effective communication. Emotions (fear, shyness, aggression) and frames of reference (bias, prejudice, experiences, assumptions, etc.) often shape communications. In addition, the current mood and life pressures on both the individual with a problem and the individual who is listening to the problem impact communication.

Business

Communication is also impacted by the policies, systems and structure within the company for which you work. For example, customers that experience long telephone wait times will have a different attitude on the phone than customers that waited a very short time on the telephone before their call was answered.

Situational

The environment in which you work, and the surrounding circumstances, may also be barriers to effective communication. For example, the time of day when a call is answered could be a factor in communications (e.g. during a hectic lunch hour). Also the temperature in the workplace, the noise volume in the room you work in, the number of intrusions and interruptions, etc. can impact communication.

A few specific examples of barriers to communication

- Your customer's primary language may not be English. Your business wants to sell to all potential customers to maximize profits. This could make communicating a challenge. Do not get frustrated. Know your co-workers. You may have one who can communicate with your customer better. If you do not, do your best.

- Your customer and you may have different levels of education, and use different words in normal conversations. Use your active listening skills (attention, repeating, summarizing) to ensure that your customer understands you, and that you truly understand your customer.

- Avoid using jargon, even when dealing with internal customers. It becomes very easy to use words that are common in your workplace, but are not part of the general public's vocabulary. If I were to tell you that every business owner should enroll in "S.E.E.K.", you would have no idea what I meant. Instead, if I said that every business owner should enroll in the Palm Beach County Resource Center's entrepreneurship training program where participants learn while creating work product for their businesses, you would have a better idea what I meant. While saying "S.E.EK." saves me a lot of words, there would have been no comprehension from the person to whom I was speaking.

- Be sure you speak in clear language to avoid any double-meanings or uncertainty in your statements to customers. Double-meanings are great for jokes, but customer service is serious business!

- Unfortunately, personalities are part of every exchange with customers. Some people handle stress well, while others do not. Some people react calmly to problems, while others do not. And some people just rub other people the wrong way for no real reason. These situations can get in the way of communicating with your customers. You cannot allow that to happen. Be aware of these situations when they arise. Know that they are unavoidable in customer service roles, and that they happen to everyone. Therefore, do not take these situations personally. Be professional and ignore the personality conflicts and concentrate on understanding and resolving your customers' problems.

- Sometimes business policies can hinder your communications with customers. Know those policies because it will help you understand how to deal with those situations. For example, a customer may have bought an item at "final sale prices" and that may mean no returns. If the customer didn't know that and tries to return the item, it could lead to a misunderstanding and an escalation of the problem if you did not know that policy either.

- Often work conditions add to the difficulty in communicating with customers. If there is construction going on in your office, the noise could make it hard to hear customers you are talking to on the phone. So, while you may not normally use headphones when talking on the phone, you may need to use them until the construction is completed.

- Customers may have experience a long wait, or the run-around before getting to you. Therefore, they could start off demanding and impatient. Get beyond their impatience and solve their problems.

To summarize: the best way to ensure that communication between your customer and yourself goes well is to be prepared by knowing your job well, using your active listening skills, using a friendly tone at all times even if your customer is not, and assuming that you will have to overcome communication problems or communication shortcomings.

Personal Signals

Personal signals were covered in detail in the chapter Communications in the *People Skills* section. Personal signals are non-verbal communication. They are your voluntary and involuntary facial and body movements that are in play as you communicate with others.

So be aware of the personal signals you are broadcasting. You may say the right thing but if your body language is saying something else, you will be sending mixed signals. You can also use those always present personal signals to your advantage. By reading the personal signals of the individual you are talking to, you can tell if he/she comprehends what you just told him/her. A puzzled look goes a long way in letting you know you will have to find different words to explain what you just said again. I do that all the time when I teach my entrepreneurship course. If I see looks of comprehension, I go on to the next topic, on the rare occasion I see some looks of confusion, I go over the topic again, presenting it in a different way.

For an in depth look at personal signals, including a list of some positive and negative personal signals, see the *People Skills'* chapter on communications.

EXERCISE CS11

Whose Line is it Anyway personal signal exercise

Q1: Just like the television show where the catch phrase is where everything's made up and the points don't matter. That's because this is an improvisational exercise and there is no grade so the points don't matter.

Wait for instructions from your instructor; and have fun.

*****

Communicating with Customers

What follows are some skills that will help you become a superior provider of customer service, which will result in you becoming a valuable asset to your employer. As you read through this section, think about situations where you have interacted with businesses whose employees made some mistakes regarding these skills. Then think about the image these employees gave of their companies.

Choosing words

You call my company DTR Inc. and want to talk to me. The employee who answers the phone responds, "Mr. Goldberg is still on his break. I'll have him call you when he gets back."

What impression does this response give you?

Let's try another. Again, you call my company to talk to me. The employee on the phone responds, "Mr. Goldberg is not back from lunch yet. I'll have him call you when he gets back."

What impression does this response give you?

We'll try this one more time. You call, this time the employee who answers says, "Mr. Goldberg is busy, can he call you later?"

How would you feel if you got this response?

I don't know about you, but in the first case I would have the impression that Mr. Goldberg is taking an extended break. In the second case, I would get the impression that Mr. Goldberg was expected back from lunch earlier and is late reporting back to work from lunch. In the third case, I would feel that Mr. Goldberg does not value me as a customer. After all he is busy with something else, but I have a problem, and he should be dealing with me; at least enough to talk to me quickly.

Choosing words worksheet (done during lecture)

How would you re-word what the employee said to correct these negative impressions?

What was said: Mr. Goldberg is still on his break.

Corrected: _____

What was said: Mr. Goldberg is not back from lunch yet.

Corrected: _____

What was said: Mr. Goldberg is busy, can he call you later?

Corrected: _____

I'll give you my take on these statements in a bit. However, I want to add two more employee/customer interactions for you to consider.

A customer who had a serious problem calls you. The Problem Resolution Department completed working on the customer's problem an hour ago, and in addition to putting in a fix on the customer's account ensuring that the situation would not happen again, they refunded money to the customer's account.

When the customer calls you inform that customer that he or she is getting a refund and that the Problem Resolution Department made changes to the customer's account so that the problem should not occur again.

See anything wrong here?

Obviously, I do or I wouldn't ask the next question. How would you change that response?

_____

_____

_____

_____

Let me give you another example of "words gone wrong."

A customer calls in with a major problem. After taking in all the information, the employee responds, "You should be hearing from us within five days."

How would you change this response?

_____

_____

_____

_____

Now that you had time to think about the prior examples of employee/customer interactions, let's see what was done incorrectly by the employee.

When interacting with customers (both internal and external) it is very important to watch the words that you use. Words like, "still, yet, busy, should" need to be avoided. For example:

Mr. Goldberg is "still" on his break gives the impression that he is late coming back from break. That is not a positive image to create for the customer.

Mr. Goldberg is not back from lunch "yet" gives the impression he is late coming back from lunch. That is not a positive image to create for the customer.

Mr. Goldberg is "busy" can he call you later gives the impression that what he is doing is more important than spending time with the person who wants to speak to him. That is not a positive image to create for the customer.

In all these cases the best response is a simple, *"Mr. Goldberg is unavailable; how may I help you?"*

One of the biggest no-no's in customer service is the use of the phrase, "Your problem 'should' be resolved now." Should is a wishy-washy, weak, leaving room for not coming through word in these cases. If I were the customer, use of the word "should" would get me angry and invoke a response like, "Should, should, what do you mean should? It better be resolved." The proper response is, "Your problem is now resolved."

So in the previous example, the wording needs to be "so that the problem *will* not occur again." Please, don't use "should not occur" again.

The same is true with timeframes. You "should be" hearing from us within five days." Again, say, "You *will* be hearing from us within five days."

While some of you will just need to watch your words, others will have to be careful not to give too many details. These are customers, not personal friends.

For example, "Mr. Goldberg left early to meet with his divorce attorney." Unless we're buds and you think the caller is someone I could be interested in dating, this is too personal a response for the caller. In fact, even if you think I could be interested in the caller it is too personal. Again, just say, *"Mr. Goldberg is unavailable, may I help you?"*

Another doozie I've heard is, "Mr. Goldberg can't talk to you now; he's in an important meeting with Senior Management working on a major problem that a very important client has encountered. Can he call you back as soon as he's out of that meeting?" Huh? First of all it is a horrible idea to tell a customer that the company has a major customer problem. It's none of their business. Second, what is this customer; chopped liver? This customer will feel he/she is as important as any other customer so his/her problem should get the same immediate attention as the supposedly "very important client." Once again, a simple, *"Mr. Goldberg is unavailable, may I help you?"* will suffice.

Even the word, "may" can, at times, be a weak word. For example, I apologize for the inconvenience this "may" have caused you. In this case, "may" is a terrible word. If the customer was not inconvenienced, he/she will not care if the word "may" is used or not. However, if the customer <u>was</u> <u>inconvenienced</u> "may" sounds like you are belittling what he/she went through. So always say, *"I apologize for the inconvenience this has caused you."* This works for both customers who were and who were not inconvenienced.

EXERCISE CS12

Point out why the following statements are not appropriate for the workplace (some contain more than one reason why it is a poor statement). Then re-write them so that they are appropriate and do not reflect poorly on the company or the individuals involved.

Q1. Mr. Dean is not back from his meeting with his son's criminal attorney. I don't know when he will be back, but I'll have him call you as soon as he can.

Q2. I'm glad you called us about your that problem. As it turned out it impacted about half of our customers. But, we should have it under control now.

Q3. Ms. Dean is busy talking with Roland from the Tet Corporation. That is our most important client. So I'll try to help you the best I can. If I cannot help, please be patient and I'll have Ms. Dean call you as soon as he can.

Q4. I know we missed your deadline. Therefore, our next delivery will be free. I am sorry for the inconvenience this may have caused you.

Q5. Jake had to leave early and to take his pet, Oy, to the vet. Can I help you?

Q6. I am sorry that you haven't heard from the billing department yet, but they are backlogged. However, you should hear from them within the next 24 hours.

Q7. Mr. Dean is not in yet. Can I help you?

*****

Classifying customer statements

Active listening is a key skill in helping you determine if a customer (internal or external) statement to you is a comment, a question, or an objection. Many providers of service turn a one minute customer session into a ten minute hassle by misinterpreting a comment as an objection. Others breed customer dissatisfaction by misinterpreting a question as a comment and, therefore, never addressing that question. Perhaps worst of all is when a provider of service (or a salesperson) misinterprets an objection as a statement. In a service scenario, the customer interaction will never end satisfactorily for the customer until the objection has been addressed. That's hard to do if the provider of service never "hears" the objection. In a sales scenario, if the salesperson does not "hear" a customer's objection he/she cannot overcome it, and he/she will not make the sale.

Let's look at some examples.

1) "Your prices are higher than I thought they would be"

This is an objection. You must first address the fact that the customer believes the prices are too high before proceeding. A response could be, "I hope that won't be a problem. Our products are the best in the business. May I show you some?" If you never address the objection, the customer will never consider purchasing your products.

2) "My computer is broken"

This is a statement. If you interpreted this as an objection (something you had to overcome to continue with the customer) you may have responded with a statement such as, "We have an excellent track record with our computers. We have the best service record in town." The customer might then respond, "Not with me…" and then either get into an argument with you over your company's service record, or worse, say, "Not with me, maybe I'll check out your competition!"

If you correctly classified this as a statement, your response would have been, "Tell me what's wrong so we can get it fixed right away." This avoids a long, unnecessary discussion.

3) "How do I use this feature"

This is a question. If you do not answer it by showing the customer how to use the feature, your customer will not be satisfied.

EXERCISE CS13

Identify whether the following are statements, questions or objections.

Q1. I think your service is the best in the business
Q2. Why was I charged a service fee
Q3. Your selection of pipes is insufficient
Q4. You delivered the wrong product
Q5. When will you have Boston Terriers in stock
Q6. I need the product immediately
Q7. I refuse to pay that bill

*****

Overcoming objections

Use the following four-step process to overcome objections:

1. Use your active listening skills to hear what the customer is saying.

2. Provide an immediate response that addresses the customer's objection.

3. Talk in a concise, clear and positive manner.

4. Don't provide unnecessary information and conversation.

Proper Telephone Technique

There are certain procedures that are fairly universal when answering a telephone call from a customer. They are:

1. Greet the caller by stating the name of your company, your name and "how may I help you."

2. Use a friendly, cheerful tone when answering the phone.

3. Never place a caller on hold without first giving the caller a chance to respond. In other words, do not follow up the greeting in number one with "hold please" and then place the caller on hold.

4. While talking with a customer on the phone, ask them if you can place them on hold (e.g. "I need to look that information up on my computer, can I place you on hold for a moment?")

5. Do not leave the customer on hold for a long time. Check back with the customer every minute or two to provide a status (e.g. I am still working on your problem; I will have your answer shortly).

6. If you did not do this earlier: Look at your watch or a clock and write down an exact time (including seconds).

Then sit and do not look at the clock, do not count or do anything else to help track how much time passes. Then look at your watch or clock again when you believe two minutes have passed. This will give you an idea how customers are experiencing the time.

7. It is also important to take notes when performing customer service functions. After one day we forget 46% of what we heard, after 7 days we forget 65% of what we heard, after 14 days we forget 79% of what we heard.

Managing Customers

Customers are people. You come across all kinds in life, and you will on your job as well. What follows are suggestions on how to handle different types of customers. While this will help in the workplace, it can also help you in every day life.

<u>The demanding, determined customer who is speaking very strongly and wants immediate action.</u>

Steps to follow:
1. Use your active listening skills to identify the problem correctly.
2. Even though the customer may be worked-up, remain friendly and courteous.
3. React only to the problem, not the customer's tone. The customer is not mad or angry at you, just at the situation. Do not take it personally.
4. Ask the customer questions about the situation, and using your active listening skill of repetition, repeat some of the customer's key words back to him/her.
5. After you understand the customer's problem, use your active listening skill of summation, to re-state the problem in short, to-the-point sentences.
6. Communicate your understanding of the importance of this issue to the customer.

The laid-back customer who has a serious problem, but is an ineffective communicator causing you problems in getting all the details.

Steps to follow:
1. Draw the customer out by asking a lot of questions.
2. Use your active listening skill of summation often and ask the customer to comment on your summary.
3. Make the customer feel comfortable by remaining warm and friendly throughout the entire conversation (if you are getting frustrated by the customer's lack of communication skills, do not show that frustration).

The chatty customer (also known as the "Energizer Bunny customer" because they go on and on and on) who views you as both a person who will solve his/her problem, and a person to engage in general conversation.

Steps to follow:
1. Only ask questions about the customer's problem and ask specific questions (not general, open-ended questions). For example, "Tell me why your stereo is not working", not, "Tell me what's wrong."
2. Talk in long bursts and leave little time between statements, making it harder for the customer to jump in to interject personal comments.
3. Be careful not to be rude. You may think that the person has no concern for you since he/she is stopping you from doing your job, but you cannot let that show. He/she is a customer and customers are the reason you have a job. So stay friendly and courteous.
4. Provide very short responses to off-topic questions. Be sure not answer in a way that leaves the door open for a long comment by the customer. Remember; do not be rude by ignoring the customer. Let's say the customer is

buying a music CD and asks you who you like. Answer with a popular band who the customer is likely to know (an unknown will result in follow-up questions) and finish by asking a yes-no question that has no where else to go. For example, "I like U2, do you need anything else today?"

The furious customer who does not cross the line in terms of language (does not curse), but is coming close and does have a legitimate problem.

Steps to follow:
1. Apologize for the problem. Remember do not use the word "may" when apologizing. Say, "I apologize for the inconvenience this has caused you."
2. No matter what, remain friendly and courteous. Again, the anger is about the situation even though it appears to be focused on you.
3. Use your active listening skills to identify and to restate the problem. In this case it is very important that you identify the correct problem or the customer's anger will grow.
4. Be sure that you have resolved the customer's problem, and that you have communicated the solution effectively to the customer.
5. Once the problem is resolved, repeat step one. Apologize again.

If a customer crosses the line and curses, you can tell him/her that you do not have to listen to that and if he/she continues you will call security (or report the customer to your supervisor). That usually works, you get an apology and the rest of the conversation is often much easier. If the customer continues to use foul language, call security, or report the customer to your supervisor. Also, if a customer shows any physical aggression, do not even try to handle it yourself. Call security or the police.

Consumer Rights

As a provider of customer service you should be aware of the rights of your customers. What follows is information taken from the Consumer Protection Act.

"Be it enacted by the Senate and House of Representatives of the United States of America in Congress assembled, that this Act may be cited as the "Consumer Protection Act of 1997.

STATEMENT OF FINDINGS AND PURPOSES

Sec. 2 (a) The Congress finds that the interest of consumers are inadequately represented and protected within the Federal Government and that vigorous representation and protection of the interest of consumers are essential to the fair and efficient functioning of a free market economy. Each year, as a results of this lack of effective representation before Federal agencies and courts, consumers suffer personal injury, economic harm, and other adverse consequences in the course of acquiring and using goods and services available in the marketplace.

(b) The Congress therefore declares that-

(1) A non-regulatory governmental organization to represent the interest of consumers before Federal agencies and courts could help the agencies in the exercise of their statutory responsibilities in a manner consistent with the public interest and with effective and responsive government. It is the purpose of this Act to protect and promote the interest of the people of the United States as consumers of goods and services which are made available to them through commerce or which affect

commerce by so establishing an independent Agency for Consumer Advocacy.

(2) It is the purpose of the Agency for Consumer Advocacy to represent the interest of consumers before Federal agencies and courts, receive and transmit consumer complaints, develop ad disseminate information of interest to consumers, and perform other functions to protect and promote the interest of consumers. The authority of the Agency to carry out this purpose shall not be construed to supersede, supplant, or replace the jurisdiction functions, or powers of any other agency to discharge its own statutory responsibilities according to law.

(3) It is the purpose of this Act to promote protection of consumers with respect to the-

(A) safety, quality, purity, potency, healthfulness, durability, performance, repair ability, effectiveness, truthfulness, dependability, availability, and cost of any real or personal property or tangible or intangible goods, services, or credit;

(B) preservation of consumer choice and a competitive market;

(C) price and adequacy of supply of goods and services;

(D) prevention of unfair or deceptive trade practices;

(E) maintenance of truthfulness and fairness in the advertising, promotion and sale by a producer, distributor, lender, retailer or other supplier of such property goods, services, and credit;

(F) furnishing of full, accurate, and clear instructions, warnings and other information by any such supplier concerning such property, goods, services, and credit;

(G) protection of the legal rights and remedies of consumers; and

(H) providing of estimates of the cost and benefits of programs and activities established by Federal Government regulations and legislation.

(4) It is the purpose of Section 24 of this Act to establish a means for estimating in advance the consumer cost and benefits of Federal legislation or rules that have substantial economic impact, and to prevent the adoption of Government programs whose costs to consumers outweigh their benefits.

(5) This Act should be so interpreted by the executive branch and the courts so as to implement the intent of Congress to protect and promote the interests of consumers, and to achieve the foregoing purposes."

EXERCISE CS14

Answer the following questions true or false.

Q1. When dealing with a demanding customer, react only to the customer's words, not the customer's tone.
Q2. To overcome a customer objection, change the topic of the discussion to get past the objection.
Q3. When you have to do work on your computer to help solve a customer's problem, leaving them on hold for 10 or 15 minutes straight with no interaction from you is fine, as long as when you come back to them you have resolved the problem.
Q4. Consumer rights is something enacted by the U.S. Congress.
Q5. When you answer the phone at work, providing your name to the caller is optional, it is not part of standard procedures for properly answering the phone.

Q6. When dealing with a chatty customer who likes to talk to you about things not relating to the company or the reason for the call; it is a good idea to talk continuously so that you do not provide a dead period where the customer can chime in with unnecessary, off-topic talk.

Q7. Active listening skills cannot help you when trying to manage difficult customers.

Q8. When you get an angry caller, the first thing you should do is apologize for the problem or situation without using weak words.

*****

Certification Scenarios

Customer Service Scenario 1

Help Us Help You, Inc. just completed its first round of in-depth customer research regarding its service delivery. The research included both surveys and focus groups. Many reports were generated highlighting both the good and the bad regarding the company's customer service. You have been invited to a strategic planning meeting to discuss the findings and to help decide steps Help Us Help You Inc. needs to take to improve its service delivery.

Lauren has been put charge of the strategic planning session and starts off by stressing the importance of providing superior customer service. Right away Anne jumps in and says, "Why did we spend over $100,000 on this study? Our products and services are the best in the marketplace and that's what drives our business. As far as I am concerned if we offered no customer service we would still sell a lot." Lauren seems taken by surprise and answers, "I know we have great products and services. This is something management wants so let's just do this the best we can."

Lauren continues, "One of the most interesting findings from the study was that a portion of our customers are complaining about something we fixed three years ago. In fact, our fix is what has propelled our product to the top of *Consumer Report* lists." Mr. K says, "They're fools. Ignore them." Ryan chips in with, "Mr. K, how is that different from how you treat all our customers?" Mr. K just smiles.

Lauren, addressing Mr. K, says "Is that true, do you ignore all our customers?" Mr. K smiles and says, "Not usually."

Owen then says, "Isn't this a meeting about our customers. Let's get back on track. I have things to do after the meeting." Lauren says, "You're right. Let's talk about what our customers want. The research shows that they want a price point 20% below our current prices; thoughts anybody?"

Ryan says, "Just because they want lower prices doesn't mean we have to give them that. Everyone wants lower prices. Our sales have been increasing every month at the current prices."

Danny follows up with, "I thought we wanted to be a customer-focused organization. Doesn't that mean give the customers what they want? Let's cut the prices."

Ryan responds," Being customer focused doesn't mean give them everything they want. That's just silly. What if they want you to go to their house and cook them dinner." Mr. K jumps in with, "I've done that."

Ryan continues, "Do you even know what cutting the prices will do to the profit margin; we could lose money on every sale."

Mr. K jumps in again and says, "Yeah, but even if you're right Ryan, we'll sell more products that way."

Lauren says, "Danny and Ryan, you both make good points. Let's table this topic until later. I now want to discuss another thing our customers indicated they wanted. They indicated that they would like music on hold instead of dead air like we currently have. They indicated that they never know if they are still on hold or if the call has been dropped. This was a very big negative that came out of the study. Our phone system can do this easily and it costs us nothing. What do you think?"

George says, "Seems reasonable. They want it, we can do it, and it costs nothing." Lauren, looking at Anne, asks, "Any objections?" Mr. K raises his hand. Lauren, "Yes, Mr. K?" Mr. K says, "I could sing live to the customers on hold." Ryan says, "Mr. K, we want to attract more customers, not drive them away." Lauren concludes, "Done deal, we'll implement music for customers on hold."

Lauren continues, "Now I have to talk about a sensitive topic. Management wants me to install service measurements. This includes ongoing customer surveys, reports by departments, and individual productivity measurements. I'm going to hand out the list of measurements now."

After handing out the list, and giving the group time to review the list, Lauren asks, "Any questions?"

Anne jumps in with, "Why are you measuring the time it takes me to generate the report I give to Yolanda? Our customers don't read the report."

Ryan says, "Yes, but the report contains information Yolanda needs to better understand how our products are used. This helps her when she gets questions from customers."

Anne says, "Ryan, I'm not talking to you." Yolanda then says, "Anne I use the report to better understand how our products are used. This helps me when I get questions from customers."

Anne just sighs.

Lauren, "Anne, that sigh of yours came up in our study as well."

Anne, "What do you mean? How come I was mentioned at all?"

Lauren, "Remember that survey you took on working with other employees; that was part of the customer service study."

Mr. K raises his hand. Lauren, "Yes, Mr K." Mr. K responds, "Yes, I remember."

Shaking her head from side to side, Lauren continues, "Your co-workers indicated that you are difficult to work with because of your negative attitude. That sigh is an example."

Anne says, "I understand that, but what does that have to do with customer service. I don't do that when I interact with customers."

Lauren responds, "That's true, you are good with our customers. I guess management is concerned that if you act that way with your co-workers that maybe that will carry over to your communications with our customers. I'm not really sure, just watch it."

Lauren continues, "One more topic to discuss, and then we'll call it day." Mr. K, "Can I call it Fred instead?"

Ignoring Mr. K, Lauren says, "As far as our employees are concerned, our Phone Center Staff were the most dissatisfied in their jobs. They believe their supervisor, Steven, and his assistant manager, Carrie, are on a power trip and treat them like kids. They feel this way because they are scheduled for lunch, cannot come in late, even a minute to work, and are watched very closely. You know that a report comes out every day that indicates the percent of time they were plugged into the system, their average talk time; and the number of calls they work on every day. This is a serious issue."

Fausta asks, "Why does Steven and Carrie treat them like that. That's not right."

Anne jumps in and says, "Wait a minute. They are just employing good phone center management techniques. In fact, they are being very customer-focused, which is what this meeting is all about anyway. If you want, Lauren, I can talk to them and explain why Steven and Carrie treat them like that. It could be better coming from someone outside their department. Oh, and I'll watch my "sighs.""

Lauren responds, "That would be great Anne. Thanks. Meeting adjourned."

Mr. K. says, "Can I stay another 15 minutes?" However, everyone was already gone.

Customer Service Scenario 2

Hive Mind Inc. is a very busy company with many employees. Below is how the day has been going for some of those employees.

Peter works in phone center as a customer service representative. Having worked in customer service for ten years, Peter has his own ideas regarding customer service. He believes customers need to chill. He is very good at his job and is able to meet their needs. He also feels that after he understands a problem he can work better without them yammering in his ear. So he puts them on hold to get peace and quiet and leaves them on hold until he finishes his work on their problem. This can take up to six minutes, which is twice as fast as most of his co-workers.. Peter also believes that customers should not get the run around. So he studies hard and learns how to fix all kinds of problems so he can deal with all customer problems without having to transfer the call to anyone else. Customers expect a lot, thinks Peter, but that's okay, they should. After all they should not have had problems in the first place.

Peter's office is located in South Florida where many of the company's customers speak Spanish. Unfortunately, Peter does not speak nor understand Spanish. Peter reports to work at 11:00 AM right before the high-volume lunch hour. Before Peter reports to his workstation he notices that three co-workers are out today. This is going to make for a very busy day since the calls will be backed up. As he sits down Peter notices the sign on the blackboard that says, feel free to take off your jackets and ties, the air conditioner is not working. Boy, talk about making a difficult situation even worse! After answering three calls, Peter's supervisor, sits down next to him and says, "Peter, our customer statements that went out last week had errors in them. All our customers are going to see a $1,000 charge that is not a real charge." Boy, Peter thinks this day is getting tougher and tougher.

Peter's fourth call of the day is from an angry, aggressive caller who won't stop complaining about the $1,000 charge. Peter tries to interrupt but the caller just keeps on complaining about the charge. If only the customer would slow down and listen, Peter could tell him that there was an error and the $1,000 charge is being removed from the account. The caller keeps going on and on and on and on. Finally, Peter tunes him out. Three minutes later Peter hears the customer saying, so what are you going to do about it being broken. Peter has no idea what the customer is talking about.

In another part of the building is Peter's kid brother Andrew. Andrew is talking in person to a customer. Watching him very closely is his supervisor, Hyrum. Hyrum notices that Andrew is listening more than talking. When he does say something Andrew often uses some of the words and phrases that the customer just said. Hyrum then notices Andrew start to talk. In fact he just summarized very succinctly the information the customer just told him. In addition, Andrew looks very interested in what the customer is saying. If he didn't know better, Hyrum thinks, Andrew looks as interested in this conversation as he is playing his video games.

Back in the phone center where Peter works, sits his sister Valentine. When the phone rings Valentine says, "How may I help you?" The customer on the phone says to Valentine, "You're company is the worst I have ever dealt with. But you sound nice. Hey, have you ever read the book *Ender's Game*? It's a great book. You must read it. Let me tell you about it."

The next call Valentine gets is from a customer who is very demanding, who wants immediate action. This customer says, "Your delivery men ripped the couch I just had delivered."

Next up is a very angry customer. This customer says, "I do not understand this charge. Why did I get it?"

That call from the very angry customer is followed by a call from a customer who appears on verge of apologizing for having a problem. The customer seems very reluctant to talk about the problem. However, it is a very serious problem and Valentine needs to know more because this problem could be impacting other customers.

In the backroom observing the ongoing customer service is Bean, the new management trainee. As he is witnessing the various acts of service, Hyrum is sitting next to him quizzing him all the time.

The first call Bean observes is Petra calling one of her clients and asking him if there was anything he needed.

Next Bean observes Tom taking a call from an upset customer. However, by the end of the call, the customer was thanking Tom and he no longer seemed upset.

After that call concluded, Bean listens in on the Production Manager, Dink, congratulating Han and his team for their latest run because it had no defects.

For his last monitoring session Bean listens in on Bonzo and his team talking about enhancements needed to the latest product. Bean also notices that Andrew, part of Bonzo's team, is not in the room.

Later Bean finds out that Bonzo sent Andrew to get coffee for the group. It seems that Bonzo is always excluding Andrew. Boy, thinks Bean, one day that situation is going to come to a head.

The Author's Training Philosophy

When I was hired to develop a work readiness curriculum in 2002 there were already a number of established work readiness training programs. With employers complaining about the lack of job skills and poor workplace behaviors by their employees in focus groups throughout the United States, I knew I had to develop more than a training curriculum; I needed to create a better way to deliver workplace training.

First, let's look at traditional programs.

Traditional Programs

Practically all workplace training programs follow models used in education. That means that they are assessment based. FCAT, SAT, etc., determine success in education and, similarly, a certification test determines success in many workplace training courses. And once workplace training ends there is no formal process to hold the individuals trained accountable for what they learned during training.

In fact, assessment tests have become so important in education that schools not only teach students knowledge, but teach students how to take tests. They must. After all, funding is often tied to their students' performances on tests such as the FCAT. Certainly many high school juniors and seniors enroll in courses to help them learn how to improve their SAT scores. And this is not just the case with kids. How many construction management schools, real estate schools, and even schools to help with the BAR exam for attorneys are out there? These schools often teach their students how to take and pass tests.

What does this mean? It means that if a student truly knows only 55% of the required knowledge, but can reduce the other questions to a possible 1 in 3 choice, the laws of probability conclude that the student's expected result on the test is 70%.

Even worse, if a student truly knows only 60% of the required knowledge, but can reduce the other questions to a possible 1 in 2 choice, the laws of probability conclude that the student's expected result on the test is 80%. That means a student whose knowledge base is an "F" (60% was failing grade when I went to school), appears to be a "B" student.

While educators cling to the argument that assessment tests are good indicators of success, no one can make that case when dealing with job skills and behaviors. As an example let's use the following multiple choice question:

If you wake up in the morning and your car will not start, you should:

A) Have made prior arrangements with a coworker who lives in your neighborhood to serve as an emergency ride to work.

Whether because of actual knowledge or eliminating answers like, "B) Take as many days off of work as you need to get your car fixed," someone answering this question correctly does not mean that that is the behavior he or she will follow if this situation actually happened to him or her. Workplace training is NOT about answering questions correctly. It's about doing the right thing in the workplace. That is accomplished through training materials that not only teach what is expected in the workplace, but *why* that skill/behavior is important in the workplace; and also uses real life examples that everyone can relate to outside of the workplace to help illustrate key points. In workplace training, it is the journey (curriculum) that is the key, not the final destination (assessment test). This is because success is measured in the attitudes changed and instilled in participants, not on how much work readiness knowledge they possess.

While this may be obvious to you and me, it isn't obvious to the powers that be. For example, instead of investing in a structured program with an effective curriculum that would produce high-quality employees that employers could rely on; many states either independently or in groups decided to spend funds on generating work readiness credentials through assessment testing. They appear to care more about formulating the perfect question, than the perfect learning tool.

Work readiness certification test results from programs that do not have effective curriculum that changes and shapes attitudes, are, at best, an indicator for possible success and, at worst, a false hope for the business community that hires the "credentialed graduates."

Jay Goldberg's Workplace Training Philosophy

I have been developing and fine-tuning my workplace training program and philosophy since 2002. What follows is a list of the key components for what I know is the correct way to implement a workplace training program.

(1) The client for employee training programs is the **business community** first, and the classroom participants second. Why? Employers observing the participants in the workplace will ultimately determine if the training program is successful; not

how well the participants perform in class or on tests. In addition, if employers like the program and believe they can rely on the participants who successfully complete the training to perform well in the workplace; they will value, hire and promote graduates of the program. And that is the main reason the participants are taking the training; to get jobs, keep jobs, and grow in their jobs. In other words, participants want to increase their value to employers.

This realization separates the training programs developed and implemented by the author from most of the other programs in the marketplace. Schools (for sure) and most other venues as well, take on the strategy to improve their students as much as possible, and then market them as vigorously as they can to the marketplace. The result is often graduates, who the school/ training venue expect may fall short of expectations, getting hired and, in fact, falling short of expectations. This result hurts future graduates of the program.

Therefore, my workplace training programs do not allow participants to achieve full certification unless they demonstrate that the main client (the business community) will be able to rely on them at work.

(2) A curriculum that not only teaches what is expected, but why that skill/behavior is important in the workplace, and uses real life examples that everyone can relate to outside of the workplace to illustrate key points, is the foundation to having a successful workplace training program. By clearly defining important workplace skills and behaviors, and informing participants why those skills and behaviors are important to employers; the program sets a baseline of understanding and helps change the participants' attitudes and behaviors.

(3) The training needs to be run like a place of business not a typical educational classroom. The instructor is not just the trainer, but during training is the supervisor, and the participants treat each other as co-workers, not training buddies or friends.

(4) After taking workplace training courses, exams (certification exams or otherwise) are used NOT to indicate competency, but to demonstrate that the participants understood the concepts taught during training so that their employers can start holding them accountable for demonstrating those competencies on the job.

(5) Since performance on the job is what is important to employers, the key program assessments are not the exams, but demonstrated competencies the participants prove every day in class. This also helps the participants understand how they will be evaluated on the job. As an example, during training, a participant demonstrates the ability to not be tardy by never being late to a training session and never extending breaks during a training session.

(6) Since certified program graduates will have shown that they understand the concepts taught during training, and that they can follow some simple, basic rules that are employed during training (through demonstrated competencies); employers should be encouraged to incorporate the competency statements in the training program into their employees' formal performance appraisals.

(7) Within the training program, all competency statements must be very well defined. There should be no leeway given to individual trainers in scoring pass/fail on competencies.

(8) Hold the participants accountable for meeting <u>all</u> their competencies. Recommend to the employers you work with to help place your graduates, that they tie individual compensation (raises, bonuses, etc.) and individual/work unit rewards (employee of the month, monthly pizza party, etc.) to their employees' performances in meeting their competencies.

(9) In addition to training participants, if there are multiple people giving the training sessions, there needs to be a consistent approach between all trainers. That means there may need to be train-the-trainer sessions to ensure all trainers conduct their training in a consistent manner. This is especially true given that the participants will be held accountable for implementing what they learn in the training session every day on the job. Knowing that everyone was trained the same way provides role models who completed the program, were hired, and are now succeeding in the workplace. And since these former program participants received the exact same training as the current participants, there are no excuses for the current participants to fail once they enter the workplace. Program consistency between trainers means no former graduate will be ale to use the excuse, "my instructor never taught me that" to their employer who hired them because of their work readiness credential.

(10) As you can see my program philosophy is very intricate and everything must work in concert to ensure optimal success. Therefore, in addition to instructor training there must be instructor audits to ensure that all teachers/trainers are following and teaching the program correctly.

Jay Goldberg's Background in Work Readiness

As mentioned previously, in 2002 I was hired to develop a work readiness curriculum that I grew into a work readiness philosophy and program. The program I developed was called the best work readiness certification program in the United States by a member of the National Skills Standard Board at a presentation of the Program in Jacksonville, Florida on 01/13/03.

The results from my initial client far exceeded those of other work readiness programs. Employers lined up to hire the graduates and found that over 85% of the graduates remained employed six months later, and over 30% received promotions.

Later I modified and added to the program for a second client.

Since that time I wrote a well-reviewed work readiness book for individuals titled, *How to Get, Keep and Be Well Paid in a Job* (Outskirts Press, ISBN: 9781432725297).

Now I have constructed a four module work readiness and customer service training program that can be used in teaching venues and for on the job training. The four modules each come with recommended competencies and a final online certification test (to use as proof of knowledge so that these individuals can now be held accountable for demonstrating what they leaned every day at work). Participants should have to pass all of the competencies in order to be eligible to sit for the certification test.

About the Author

Jay Goldberg, MBA, is a former Service Director for Citibank. At Citibank, Mr. Goldberg specialized in customer service management, measurement, training, capacity planning, profitability, MIS reporting, and strategic planning.

After almost fourteen years with Citibank, Mr. Goldberg left to form his own consulting firm, DTR Inc. DTR Inc. specializes in writing business plans, developing workplace training programs, designing and implementing customer service strategies, performing strategic planning and market research (e.g., surveys, focus groups, etc.), helping businesses build their brands, and training managers and employees.

At DTR Inc., Mr. Goldberg developed the program parameters, program strategy, curriculum, lesson plans, assessments, competency statements, and certification tests for a Work Readiness Training Program called the best Work Readiness Certification Program in the United States by a representative of the National Skills Standard Board at a presentation of the Program in Jacksonville, Florida on 01/13/03.

Mr. Goldberg later updated, modified and added to that Program for a second client and wrote a book, "How to Get, Keep and Be Well Paid in a Job" (ISBN = 9781432725297), specifically tailored to individuals looking to improve their work readiness skills.

In 2007, Mr. Goldberg was instrumental in helping the Palm Beach County Resource Center develop a revolutionary Entrepreneurship Training Program. The program's structure was unlike any other in the marketplace, and would prove to be highly successful.

In 2012, Mr. Goldberg's entrepreneurship book, "Building a Successful Business," (ISBN = 9781470000639) was published. The book is now being used as a textbook for entrepreneurship courses. The book is both a textbook and a workbook with tools entrepreneurs can use to help start, grow and manage their businesses.

While at the Palm Beach County Resource Center, Mr. Goldberg worked with hundreds of small businesses and got a good handle on how to best structure and implement a work readiness training program to ensure that the benefits of training would be demonstrated in the workplace.

In 2013 Mr. Goldberg published his book for his comprehensive work readiness and customer service training program. There is a teacher book, a classroom book (without answers) and PowerPoint presentations available in the full program.

Contact Mr. Goldberg at Book@DTRConsulting.BIZ. Be sure to write "your work readiness book" in the subject line to ensure that your email is not deleted as junk mail. His business's web site is www.DTRConsulting.BIZ.

Rock Trees: The Beatles: Volume 1: The Paul McCartney Tree
By JAY GOLDBERG

ISBN = 9781494739102

Six Degrees of Separation was originally proposed by Frigyes Karinthy. The theory says that everyone in the world can be connected through a maximum of six steps. Applying that theory to The Beatles, this book shows how 1,550 bands/artists connect back to The Beatles.

This is Volume One of a planned series and examines the Paul McCartney "Rock Tree." The other Beatles will get their own books in the future.

The book contains fifty "rock trees" each with thirty one bands/artists per tree and each with a companion chart showing how the bands are connected.

The goal was not to repeat any band/artist, although musicians can be solo artists and parts of different bands. I accomplished that goal.

Only band members or guest or studio musicians or singers were used to connect the bands/artists. Song writing, production, engineering, etc. credits did not count.

FOR MORE INFORMATION VISIT
www.createspace.com/4580254

www.ingramcontent.com/pod-product-compliance
Lightning Source LLC
Chambersburg PA
CBHW070826180526
45168CB00002B/749